DROP DEAD RED

DROP DEAD RED

Elizabeth Carmer

atmosphere press

Contents

*This book is dedicated to all those
who assisted with its publication*

Part I

Drop Dead Red

Drop Dead Red

that I could put on
that daily red lipstick

to become her
that character

not flawed
not flared

but the red
lipstick not shared

made me believe
in me for once

my mistake was thinking
my vision would be

a miracle and not
a dangerous nightmare

of me sitting waiting
for something

to make me feel
less bare

like wondering when
that tortoise

will pass that long
haired hare

A Missing Smile

how many teeth
is too many
missing teeth

like the clock
on that far
wall ticking

one two three
we know
twenty-one

is when
you can drink
sixteen

is when
you can
think

Innocence Is a Threat
So I Walked Away

that school week
was hell
I was ignorant
on purpose

trying to balance
while walking
on a railroad
track is society

I lost track
of my footing
but didn't
get stuck

to wind up dead
from anything
oncoming
only breathless

while walking
barefoot
down
that road

back to where
I'm from
trying to break free
from feeling like no one

Trying to Figure Out
How to Not Fall Down Stairs

I have broken glass
on my floor
it's not my mirror

nor my reflection
I heard it break
but it's a mistake

my mom
fell once
or twice in a house

and still lies there
like that shawl
going to my mom's

wake I imagined
she never cheated
nor had an affair nor

cut herself with that
shard but only
looked out the window

my mom
fell once
or twice in a house

and still lies there
like that shawl

looking away from glass

Just a Punk

a squatter
knows best
maybe
to beat

the heat
or head
to the air
unwashed hair

one bottle
of wine
two bottles
of wine

or three
cutters
escaping
seeing blood

choosing
to drink
not bleed
to not

defeat
themselves
in their own
bed of urine

What Color Does a Radio Wave Make?

my dad
told me
that the
siren

the fire
station
siren
wailing

went off
every day
at noon
where was I

already
born
not yet
dead

not yet
drowned
in that
brown pond

where my
sister Jessica
fell in but
was later saved

by my other
sister Lindsay
who brought
Jessica back home

deep down
I didn't
hear
that sound

of the town
every day
I drowned
it out

but do
I remember
standing
facing

the window
during
that pulsing
of sirens

which were
not grenades
not gunfire
only to stand

at that hour
to watch
and wave
with my sisters

at our grandpa

walking
by and going
back to work

Not a Zoo

down in Rio
the dead
chicken carcasses

do they smell
after a while
this is not

garbage
they were not
tortured

they are rotting
outside but not
burned alive

Baby Jessica Survived

wells dig deep
for those who have them

history feeds on them
or people cannot live

their service is not
witchcraft

and their openness
is subliminal like wealth

it's conceptual to believe
in a well

survival is ascertained
like the purveyor of a well

like that news story
of Baby Jessica found

rescued
relieved of sinking

breathing
and floating

Baby Jessica was saved
from dying inside

that tunnel or abyss
noted was its circumference

not the income of the town
this case was relieved

of the reward to find her
thank God

Balance Is Suicidal

mirror mirror
on the wall
I did not see
that fall

*

one cannot see
the ground
or that is all
that is seen

*

what is meant
what is mean
when you trust
and become dust

Miss Elizabeth

made in America is me
but I am not the bully
but I am a witness
I saw what you did
you also go by that name
no I will not say it
it is too in vain
for I am afraid of you
you stole
showed no one
and pretend to speak
in better English
you drove away
down your own path
but on a street
to your home
and you are not
my mom

An Old Adage Is Anything Coming Out of That Parrot

could we teach
the red and yellow
bird in its red
and yellow cage

to talk not
spit and not
fly into the oblivion
of its own self

this parrot
was not a watchdog
its doorbell
was a silent chirp

as a house rule
the bird is silent
supposed to be
like uninvited guests

but it chooses
to talk
not fight
its own demise

as it loses feathers
and its mind
the house is clean
but the bird so mean

The Faucet Is Dripping

is a missing
man just
a face

maybe laced
on that
old milk

carton
lying out
to dry

but many
years is too
long like rings

of a stump
of a former
tree no

longer erect
like hearing
Jane and John

Doe having
a baby or
is white

noise
trickling
through my TV

She Taught Me to Cut the Tag Off After Buying a Shirt

my mom never
had a real job
she taught
me to drive
with two feet
at all times
tap
on the accelerator
while waiting in traffic
cut the clothing tag
off
to not
be apprehended
as a stealer

To Dive or Drown

my mom
once told
me a story
that Laura
her sister
my aunt Laura
almost dove
into an empty pool
the end
of this story
is bliss
as my aunt
Laura missed
her call
to die
that day

What Is Sanitation?

a train
wreck
its
aftermath
a clandestine
cop
or
an officer
directing
traffic
where
am I
to go
when
I feel
lost
not dirty
not guilty
but not
clean

A Bird Eyeing Me

my rosary
was bought
for me

like bread
to feed
birds

innocence
to see
white

beads
preceded
the story

of my life
seeing
my imperfect

reflection
through
a window

pretending
to see
a bird

A Bird Can Only Fly
Out of the Cage
When Its Door Is Ajar

I be
pretty
one day

was a quote
I heard
a parrot
cry out

like me
I fought
but learned
that crying

out is a syringe
demeaning
my appearance
and a mirror

watching me
I see the bird
not mocking me
its eyes are senile

Part 2

The First Man and Woman

The First Man and Woman

when we think of Adam and Eve
we know of that apple

was it red or green
or does that not matter

two different contingencies
made from a single question

that create a divided world
like multiple continents

collide or collude
like the brains of Adam and Eve
who was accused

who was at fault
when did we hear

that our world
might be destroyed

Who Carries the Burden

is being relatively
wealthy a sin
or a curse

it's a description
of Mary Magdalene
like encryption

she was a witness
to an empty tomb
but as a single

lady and therefore
when she died
how did she rise

The Pronunciation
of Christopher Columbus
Is American

the United
States
of America

named after
its native
embargo

shed
diversionary
light

on the trail
of ancestry
spotted by

Europeans
named by
Foreign Affairs

and drafted
as a true
nation

drafting
its own
accord

its own

proprietary
governors

a federal
place
to collectively

bear throne
to its neighbors
like a trait

picked up
along the way
to acquiesce

one's proprietary
notion
that they won

We Speak Your Capitalism Here

like a capitalist
in a tribe
or a vanguard
acting as a mime

an aborigine
is like
a stranger
feared

not afraid
not lost
not stolen
natural

but not
preserved
sacred
forsaken

regardless
of intuition
each receives
disorder

from their
outsider
which is
not its owner

Distinct and Not Yet Extinct

like a stray
cat staring
out of its cage

when
you are human
looking out the window

what
is your
own

civil
war
its cost

is staring like a stray cat
or
birth

The Civil War De-Classified

Abraham Lincoln
came to stand
here one day

which is a thought
for most
like the backdrop

of rain
during a battle
which made

you lose
footing
victory

is gone
up in the air
the drummer boy

introduced
our flag
to its opposition

to teach
that to look
back is mimicry

like a stone
thrown
into a mud

pile
either gone
lost buried

or immortal
like our flag
which was drenched

I Haven't Read the Bible but I Do Not Swear

what
is
a
human

a person
with
or without
kids

a living
being with
or without
housing

an inmate
with
or without
parole

a body
with
or without
a gun

or this
intrepid mind
with
or without God

The Seven Deadly Sins
Include This

I see
that house
that boarder
that hoarder

it sits
on the corner
of Main Street
McConnellsville

the garbage
it occupies
the windows
facing us

no one
stops
to just
stare

except
kids
on
a dare

and one time
a rock
struck its door
like a curse

awakened
the witch
inside
a sinner

who heard
that blow
and knew
to throw

a line
of fire
down
her lair
she came
to the door
and scratched
its wood

from inside
in a raspy
voice
embodying

a stray dog
without a name
peering
at me

as if I am
bad
but

who knows

In the End
He Who Tripped and Fell

am I
superstitious
now
that I saw
Jesus
on that cross
as a mannequin
tripping
falling
as the sinner
in any land
foreign
is his crown
of thorns
I am confused
by the blood
beginning
to stream down
his face
masking
all those watching
wearing lace

The Body of Christ Was Absent

is baptism
at the age
of five
like a bucket

hanging
dry
in a well
overturned

I was baptized
at age five
I was able
to stand

and asked
to tilt
my forehead
to receive

the holy water
didn't reception
bleed salvation
no it led

to nearsightedness
how long will
this longing last
how do I find God

When to Invite a Friend
When I Feel Like an Outcast

when that bomb
went off in my head

my abandonment
is like weeping

during the day
or celebrating holidays

like the Fourth of July
that time of a nomad

calendar when bullets
fly or leftover sparks

which hit the water
can maybe hit you or me

that flyaway spark
is thinking of a socialite

Part 3

His Promise
Serves This Majesty

His Promise Serves This Majesty

did
Rumpelstiltskin
say imp
or pimp

the association
and its rhyme
only come
with a dime

not charm
not harm
its asterisk
is like a smirk

impeding
prudence
turning
straw to gold

The Golden Locks
Are Not a Noose to Hang You

what is boyish
when identifying
beauty
what is pain
when one
climbs up your hair

one could say
the earliest rhyme
was when Rapunzel
came to be
twisted fate and alas
we hear a song
out in the dry air

the tower
the climb
the height
the wait
are not
destroyed forever
by fate

Did You Know Me at First Sight

my hair turned white
and fell out

not all of it of course
I then dyed it red

to become visible
like a friend

watching not washing
that dye go down

the drain removing
me for once

Syndrome

blood poisoning
not a childhood toy
not the blue or pink attributed to birth
not zinc in the walls
a death trap between houses
girl or boy
like that time I was running
up that hill to Grandma and Grandpa's
and saw that black line in my blue vein
not a black and blue
I could have died
but what a miracle I was born

I Don't Want to Meet a Ghost

the sighting
of that ghost
while asleep
the devastating

moment
at midnight
during sleep
racing heart

sweating
is not breathing
nor escape
nor awakening

is like living in a lie
or lying awake
thinking about
a nightmare

if when awake
seeing a shadow
hearing a creak
listening

to not see
if that ghost
appears
in my door

I don't see
images

I don't
imitate

anyone
nothing
between me
and the wall

an imaginary
friend occupies
my dreams
denying this

What Is Vain When You Can't
Go By Your Own Name

is it a shame
to go by
Elizabeth

but Liz or
Beth
an audition

or a sin
my autobiography
includes these

daily psalms
of rhyming
with me

to be a Liz
is a plurality
not a mime

what's a crime
when you're
at a loss

such as when
desperation
becomes

hallucination

I walk across
that line

to meet myself
to show me
as that host

who is a silent
actress to a cast
aware

of explaining
when to be
that ghost

Living in a House
That Is Below the Usual Standard

this homelessness
is a virtue
of mine

my asylum
is not yours
to stay alive

and fight
the stigma
of your dogma

I feel
transplanted
in this space

trying
to make

       up frugality

trying to live
to breathe

      see my fight

This Transgression
Is Only for Me to See You

if called
a coward
do I still
feel

afraid
or a victim
or perhaps
just female

and which
becomes
prayer
or thought

is my subtle
personification
of this accuser
passive aggression

like those
uneducated
hypotheses
of who I am

to you
do they transfix
you before
they expire me

or is this accusation
in vain
which is only
insane

49

Heed Warning
or Fear Tape Recording

what
is your vice
anyways
mine
is committing
noise
violations

too far away
is the anchor
to this mistrust
so unmistaken
for reality
it has led
to lust

language past
used not to
abuse
has died
and created
a living nightmare
he who said
mutiny
acted out
not like us

before
you set sail
know

your vice
or vices
as those
you may
never
see
again

Alive and Awake

sleep deprivation
is not my fault
how did this happen
and how long

will this last
my appearance
will suffer
my hair

will become brittle
my heart slows
or quickens
I was spoken

to in the background
by some random
or known female
who watches me

a bedroom
not where
I grew up
but where

I have felt
incapacitated
debilitated
and alive

Part 4

American Deliverance

American Deliverance

it is a draw
or a drawing
the hold-up
is not the chain gang

loose footing
can cost
anyone
everything

so lucid
in our minds
and memories
the crime story
we read
that crime scene
we heard of

the truth
was delivered
to us

Pin the Tail on the Donkey

a donkey is a man's best friend
for it is not brain-dead
out there while walking beside
a man it tows while ignoring
the argument going on in
the center of town
searching that dust bowl
or happy ending

Your Escape

in vain
not vanity
the crowd
watches
the public
hanging

a bounty
is an overhead
climb
up
to trust in a bank
hopefully
you are liked
publicly
to get
out of this

the colonial
trade of ink
is a believable
comment
to warrant
a person
any person
guilty
if they said
what was heard

by a random person
not known
nor afraid

but deemed
the cause of your death

whispering
in a crowd
is a sign of fear
not a precursor
to a hanging
but maybe
its potential
is vivid
and makes people livid

Theory of the Blind-Sided While Acting

am I a thespian
leading the stage

or being led astray
my acting might only

be that make-up
artist's conceptual

performance
to cast me as a star

what is a mime
or even a clown

my mind begins
to wonder

and wander
and conclude

that a clown
seems more

believable
than me

To Rob a Bank
Would Never Be Capitalism

harrowing is the sun
when a bank robber
is running
from the scene of the crime

the oasis that appears
during the runaway
when the bank robber
has run and hitched a ride

acts as the broad daylight
technique of innocent
versus guilty
but his mind yells money

on that bus ride
he hears murmuring
static at all costs
above ground

away from everyone
north versus south
is not a normal route to get anywhere
the robber is allegedly trained

to get to the destination
as an incognito
where does one go
when all the money is gone

Knockout

is self-reflection
wanting
to get paid more
but how

I don't know
sitting there
while humming
and someone

walked by
didn't point
but accused me
of talking to myself

I listen
I have no meetings
I have to do things
I am cut off

I know right from wrong
teeth clattering
as people sometimes cheat
and I am not numb

like a boxer in a ring
but with no corner
it's suggested
I pretend to be dumb

That Creaking Is Not
from That Creek

that bucket
rocking
in the well
is a daydream

of mine
which
hasn't
yet

made me
famous
unlike
the voices

in my head
which I don't
have
oh well

the well
itself is alone
not whining
not wincing

amongst old
age and years
of giving
and not getting

the people
who fetch
the water
have forgotten

the paper sign
hanging
sideways reads
bad water

Are You a Puppet?

is a puppet
a theory
outside

of a classroom
only to
be defined

by its
strings cut
by a human

behind
closed doors
as master

A Debate in America

to be unoccupied
do I look back
or look forward

I expose
this cue
to follow

that magical
eight ball
in a pool

with others
calculating
disguise

A Craving Is to Cross

Tijuana
is situated
on the forefront

of an impromptu
destination
wanted dead or alive

believe
one shot
for protest

and steal
or believe
in better

and cross
the border
and not cry out

these are people
wanting to immigrate
their fate is not yet

spoken
as a person
who is in America

Part 5

Feminism
Is a Curtsy for Me

Feminism Is a Curtsy for Me

a chapel
is small
but I
am not

married
off
officially
obliging

testifying
I do
love
between

man and woman
I am gone
away from
this ring finger

my heart
didn't
die
when I lost it

a shotgun wedding
that desire
to throw
cake outside

Sugar Is Scary

cotton candy is so fun
cotton candy is for everyone
is this a cheer
is this a fight
we want you to have the same right
eat it if you dare
buy it if not scared
you must go there first
to where it is sold
like that fair

a sugar rush helps remind
you of who you saw that crush
you developed on that boy over there
that boy in line at the fair

we saw him while watching
the helium inflate the balloons
I've heard about girls who inhale that

I know he saw me I'm not daydreaming
I'll use the pay phone and tell
my babysitter to pick me up later

your mom and dad never told you
but you might have developed
a seizure disorder you cannot
eat that cotton candy

What Water Can Do

dry land is the continuation of our fight
you asked me for the canteen
while we rode horses
it was not dusk
but modern almost torturing sunlight
you hit me like an oasis for I felt despair
don't curtail obligation
and ask for water
this is not court
you drought me
and now I seek revenge
you intended to regard me as the plague
don't continue to recount our moral
duty it's inevitable that you are counterfeit
but I am not a judge

What Outfit Am I Wearing

my lab coat
while working
in the psychiatry

department
was the subject
of classification

the sterile hallway
checkered floors
blinking lights

cleaning man
with a broom
after-hours

this haunted
house housing
nothing

after parts
of me drained
I wanted to be

perfect
not confined
to that straightjacket

Hot Pink Is Not Red

a female
actress
burns
through
a script
only
to define
what
is reading
lips

How Alone Am I?

like a serial killer gnawing
at you it's

that northern cross
of that ravine

white mountains
like the aged rocks

of its frontier the mountain
knows its feet as hearth

its hang its claw are its
appearance he or she

male or female animals are all
the same only wild

hard to reach like the summit
of this cliff its cages

are human fear its caves
are human tread

a hiker knows to eat its ravine
is sunken teeth

Dry Land

some places
are higher
than others
the only real
conceptual cataclysm
is that we don't
see a volcano here
we try to look up
one day
encouraging
ourselves to make
it astray
like an ashtray
during your heyday
from a fantasy perspective
not all mountains erupt
fire and race
which is a curse
like the countenance
of my face
they too can see
I can't hide

To Agree or Disagree

the gambler who lost
said he saw a hole in his body
at the establishment
which housed a lawful game
for it became that legally
but at night it forsakes that name
and each to their own
in any casino
where fate is turned
and each to their own
one can become rawhide
gambling is the true call to honor
if you win
you can scream
like that gambler who won
was that a suicide or a counterattack
nobody knows who shot first
afterwards everyone agreed
the safety was off by mistake

To Make a Comeback

I am not a rebel
but you are a fight
we cannot break even
your harmonica plays
and drowns out the role
playing of the desert
your dirty bandana
is a cowboy rule
in a dry land
you are outlawed here
the clouds over the terrain
are clear
not smoky
like the barrel of a gun
after it shoots
your demise is the folding
doors to enter that saloon
they bounce back and hit you in the rear

This Is Not Skinny-Dipping

living on ice
is thrice
my vice

I carry
my bucket
to a hole

out there
on the ice
of Willand Pond

it's frozen
over
and will last

all winter
this time
around

I carry
my weight
without

threat
of falling
below

I carry
my stakes
to catch

any fish
not a dead
one

but my foot
catches
and I hear

a crack
the pond
is the same

I am
different
I am shaking

I go down
no one can
see me

my eyes
dart
to seeing

no fish
no living
breathing

swimming
anything
but icicles

Did You Need the Quarter
When Calling Collect?

what's invisible
maybe invincible
looking out
looking in

of a phone
booth
outside
in a lot

what's
a faster gun
when you
need to run

the telephone
book still
hangs
while

that sound
of a dial
tone
plays on

the escapee
ran
he called
collect

not to his dad
not to a friend
but as an assailant
to a stranger

but that quarter
named money
fell and hit
the ground

he robbed
that drugstore
carrying
only money

playing deaf
to hear
that stolen
quarter used

to make
a call
to make
an escape

looking behind
as he runs
through
the parking lot

only to see
only to dream
of Washington
known as silver lining

Dick and Jane Owned a Home

my grandpa's house
was like meeting Jane
for the first time

your vision
alongside my dreams
were creating your phenomenon

my true upbringing
included not regularly
swimming

I had a pond there
to speak in third person
that person rarely swam

now I am me
only I know
that trigger

that body
that person
that grave

I will not cry when you die
for you will be buried
next to Dick

dead or alive
in an outfit
               in the outdoors

What Is Gunfire?

what is an intruder
what is a tunnel

in this land deemed
drug territory

what is dancing
trying

to see
to be

partially innocent
is inescapable

but they don't clap
at a nightclub shooting

not the hysteria
of a drug bust

a dancer
can be mysterious

insinuating physically
what backfires here

is music turned off
but the interior lights

of the stage are still on
highlighting what is

movement
as an onlooker

what is spotlight
or a spotlight

what is a cover-up
or what is a stand-off

when bodies
hit cement

About Atmosphere Press

Atmosphere Press is an independent, full-service publisher for books in genres ranging from nonfiction to fiction to poetry, with a special emphasis on being an author-friendly approach to the challenges of getting a book into the world. Learn more about what we do at atmospherepress.com.

We encourage you to check out some of Atmosphere's latest releases, which are available at Amazon.com and via order from your local bookstore:

Interviews from the Last Days, sci-fi poetry by Christina Loraine

Unorthodoxy, a novel by Joshua A.H. Harris

A User Guide to the Unconscious Mind, nonfiction by Tatiana Lukyanova

The Sky Belongs to the Dreamers, a picture book by J.P. Hostetler

To the Next Step: Your Guide from High School and College to The Real World, nonfiction by Kyle Grappone

The George Stories, a novel by Christopher Gould

No Home Like a Raft, poetry by Martin Jon Porter

Mere Being, poetry by Barry D. Amis

The Traveler, a young adult novel by Jennifer Deaver

Breathing New Life: Finding Happiness after Tragedy, nonfiction by Bunny Leach

Oscar the Loveable Seagull, a picture book by Mark Johnson

Mandated Happiness, a novel by Clayton Tucker

The Third Door, a novel by Jim Williams

The Yoga of Strength, a novel by Andrew Marc Rowe

They are Almost Invisible, poetry by Elizabeth Carmer

Let the Little Birds Sing, a novel by Sandra Fox Murphy

Carpenters and Catapults: A Girls Can Do Anything Book, children's fiction by Carmen Petro

Spots Before Stripes, a novel by Jonathan Kumar

Auroras over Acadia, poetry by Paul Liebow

Channel: How to be a Clear Channel for Inspiration by Listening, Enjoying, and Trusting Your Intuition, nonfiction by Jessica Ang

Gone Fishing: A Girls Can Do Anything Book, children's fiction by Carmen Petro

Owlfred the Owl, a picture book by Caleb Foster

Love Your Vibe: Using the Power of Sound to Take Command of Your Life, nonfiction by Matt Omo

Transcendence, poetry and images by Vincent Bahar Towliat

Leaving the Ladder: An Ex-Corporate Girl's Guide from the Rat Race to Fulfilment, nonfiction by Lynda Bayada

Adrift, poems by Kristy Peloquin

Letting Nicki Go: A Mother's Journey through Her Daughter's Cancer, nonfiction by Bunny Leach

Time Do Not Stop, poems by William Guest

Dear Old Dogs, a novella by Gwen Head

Bello the Cello, a picture book by Dennis Mathew

How Not to Sell: A Sales Survival Guide, nonfiction by Rashad Daoudi

Ghost Sentence, poems by Mary Flanagan

That Scarlett Bacon, a picture book by Mark Johnson

Makani and the Tiki Mikis, a picture book by Kosta Gregory

What Outlives Us, poems by Larry Levy

Winter Park, a novel by Graham Guest

That Beautiful Season, a novel by Sandra Fox Murphy

What I Cannot Abandon, poems by William Guest

About the Author

Elizabeth Carmer continues to have a sincere interest in modern poetry, specifically wanting to incorporate her understanding of everyday life and human behavior. This latest book draws from the poet's interest in reflecting on her own past to incorporate specific times and memories to recount her upbringing. This poet writes to the point that the reader can interpret the author's intent and voice.

Elizabeth Carmer continues to work at a community health center as an administrative assistant in New Hampshire, pursuing her personal interest in public health and economics. Currently, the author is pursuing photography to capture the essence of urban landscape in order to divulge its historical implications. The author showcases her photography on her personal website https://elizabethcarmer.com.